Dare To Live:

Through Poetry

Rose Ann Goodman

To my Pap, for instilling a poet's soul in me, and my Mom, for nurturing it.

Acknowledgement

Growing up, I had a very close relationship with my maternal grandparents. My Pap was hearing and we communicated by writing, me lipreading him, and him fingerspelling. We also used some home signs, for my grandparents raised my Mom, who was also Deaf.

At the age of six, my Pap and I sat together in his lazy chair, and he taught me how to write poetry. I vividly remember him explaining and writing down how rhyming worked. It was when we wrote my very first two poems together (Pap and Barney,) and that got me started on my poetry journey. You could say that he instilled a poet's soul in me, and for that, I am forever grateful. It helped me through some of the darkest periods in my life.

My Mom was also a key figure in my poetry journey, and my biggest fan. She also wrote poetry. She unfortunately passed in 2012. She was aways asking me when I would be publishing a book of poetry. "Someday" was always my answer, and that someday has finally come. I only wish she was here to see this day. However, I believe she already has a copy in her hands in Heaven with that huge, beaming smile of hers on her face. My poem, "A Dainty Little Fairy," was her very favorite and it forever belongs to her. I love you, Mom. Always and forevermost.

To Sandy Hyman-Mehaffey, the best teacher, mentor, and friend I've ever had. I first had her as a teacher for my last two years in elementary. I remember her teaching us how to write a poem, and then she had us compose our own. "The Ocean" became my third poem. When I moved up to middle school, she got promoted to principal, and was pretty much by my side until my high school graduation. She was always supportive of my writing, and always believed in me. She was also the source of inspiration of some of my poems. Thank you, Sandy, for all the education, expriences, your support and devotion, your love, and for who you are in my life. I love you.

My dear Bernard Bragg, a big thank you, for being a beloved mentor and friend. We first met when I was 15. You took a big interest in me and my poetry. You also got me interested in Gallaudet University. It was where I learned to embrace my language, American Sign Language (ASL) and Deaf Culture, and my true identity, even though I came from a Deaf family. After truly understanding ASL and it's rules, I started producing ASL Poetry and translating poetry from English into ASL. Thank you for opening those doors.

Regarding my ASL Poetry, thank you, Dr. Ben Bahan, for believing in me, and for your support in me finishing up my

Masters' education with a degree in Deaf Studies from Gallaudet University.

To my Dad and sisters, you're my world. I love you all. Thank you for your continous support, your love, and especially your patience with me. I love you more than words can even say.

A special thank you also goes out to all of my teachers, especially those from Scranton State School for the Deaf, and Dr. Dorothy Bambach. You all played a very important role in my life in one way or another. You all are my forever family.

A thank you goes to Emma Felix, my project manager, and the Amazon Plus Publishing team for helping make this book come to fruition.

A big thank to you, my readers, for allowing me into your lives. During the course of my 40 plus years of life, I've written nearly 400 poems. It was hard selecting only 100 out of them to share with you all.

And for everyone who made their way into my poems, thank you for the inspiration and the lessons.

Life can be hard. Life can be wonderful. All we can do is DARE TO LIVE!

Pap

I spoil my Pap.

I sit on his lap.

He has no hair.

But I don't care.

He can wear my cap.

Barney

Barney is my dumb dog.

He lays on the floor like a log.

He doesn't come when you call.

Over him you will fall.

He's so fat that he really should jog.

The Ocean

I like the ocean.
Big waves, small waves.
Sea gulls flying around the sky.
Hot sand.
Sun shining.
Wind blowing.
Children playing with the sand.
Crabs crawling around.
People sun tanning.
People swimming in the ocean.
Children running around.
I love it. It is fun.

The Other Side of the World

The thrill of walking into a bookstore

Letting the books wash me ashore

Into a magical place where reading is my heart.

Letting those freshly smelling books transport

My mind from my life into others.

Respecting the books as if they are Father.

Books sitting there, screaming out; read me

Read me, read me!

All of those books stacking high with titles,

Transforming me

And transporting me into their private world,

Thus enchanting my world

Seasons

Flowers blooming.
Leaves sprouting.
Eggs cracking.
Birds singing.
It's spring.

Eating ice cream.
The warm moonbeam.
Soft breeze blowing.
School's ending.
It's summer.

The crispy air.
The trees so bare.
The wind blowing.
School's starting.
It's fall.

Animals hibernating.
White snow covering
Our frozen land
Turning it into a wonderland.
It's winter.

The seasons keep on changing.
They start out by living
And then end by dying.
Just like life.

Disturbance of Peace

The eagle, it's wings spread out,
Cruising above the wooded area.
The sweet scented pine trees
Surrounding a body of water.
The lake, several shades of blue.
The boulders sitting around the lake
As if to protect it
From the dangers in the world.
The water gently lapping
Around the shore.
The breeze gently blowing.
The warm sunshine
Encouraging plants to grow.
All was quiet and peaceful
Until a human being
Steps into the place,
Destroying it's beauty.

Silence

Sitting one on one
In an office
Staring into each other's eyes.
Her eyes boring into mine.
I quickly glance down
To play with a wadded up paper.
Glancing up at her,
I thought; say something!
I sigh.
She remains motionless
As if to watch the true me.
Unable to take it anymore,
Say something! I silently begged.
I look at her, "Say something!"
She smiles.
"The ball's in your court,"
She says.
I sigh...
Now, what?

Flying Hands

There was silence,
but the room was occupied
by flying hands.
One sign meant a thing
and the other sign meant another.
The expressions on the faces
changing quickly
to connect with the hands.
The face growing harder
as the hands moved
fast and furiously.
Then the face grows softer
as the hands dropped their pace.
The fingers,
connected to the hands,
flying in many directions.
The volume in the room
was still quiet,
but the hands
kept on flying.
Someone asked me;
"How do you communicate?"
"Look in that room, my friend,"
I said.
"Does those hands mean anything?"

Walls of Eyes

Black,
depression, death
covering me up.
Nowhere to run,
to scream...
There are dead ends
everywhere.
The walls of eyes grinning at me
as I gasp and turn
and run in another direction.
And I collide with
another grinning, menacing
wall of eyes.
Running out to the middle
of the room,
the walls of eyes
closing in onto me
until I couldn't breathe.
I squeeze my eyes shut
and open one eye fearfully.
The eyes are laughing.
"Die, you little bitch."
I scream out for help,

but it was no use.

The eyes are everywhere

and there were no room to escape.

And I become one of them,

a pair of eyes, luring someone to their death.

Nana

A kind, old lady
confined to her wheelchair.

The gleam in her eyes
is gone,
but her will to live
is so strong.

Sitting alone,
waiting for us to come.

Her smile,
always ready to greet us,
even though
her pain
may be unbearable.

The smell
of the plain, white corridor
is unfamiliar,
yet unpleasant.

As we approach her,
her eyes widen
and she clasps her hands.

Her happiness
outshining
the dreary environment.

I sit,
wondering,
what kind of life is she having now
At the nursing home?

She continues to smile,
asking us each
how we are.

A twinge of sadness
showed in her eyes.
But she continues
to keep up a brave front.

Her hands,
so thin and fragile,
clutching a Holy Bible.

As she continues
to look at us in turns
as if to memorize
our every detail.

I look at her,
feeling some pity for her.
And I think;
she had really come a long way.

And my pity
turned into admiration.
I wondered
what kind of life she led

And how fortunate I was
that she was in my life
For eighteen years.

When we stood up to leave,
I looked at her,
wondering;
Will I ever get to see her again?

I bend down to kiss her
as she held onto my hand,

not wanting to let me go.

I looked into her eyes,

sure that she was going to be OK.

"I'm so blessed that you're my great grandmother,"

I smile.

"I love you, Nana Luke."

Round and Round

Round and round
is where we are going.
Round and round
until my dizziness
has reached its' peak.
I try to steer
to a point
where we could stop
and be reasonable.
But you keep on
driving off course
with a little outburst here
and an outburst there.
I clamp my mouth shut
in frustration
as I try to keep
the car in control.
You kept on
distracting me
until I totally lost
my concentration
and we crash into a wall.
The blames were being
put on me

"See what you did.

It was your fault."

I raise my hand

to strike you,

but my conscience

would not allow me.

I uttered a cry,

and let it all out,

hoping that you would listen.

And when I thought

I had gotten through to you,

we pulled out

and started driving again.

And we went

nowhere,

but round and round

and round and round.

Mirror of Suicide

The mirror of you,
crumbling to pieces.
As your mind
proceed to do the same.
The emotional valve
in your eyes loosens
and a dam breaks out.
As a rush of air
whirlwinds through your head,
leaving a mess behind.
You grab a piece
of the deadly glass,
holding your arm out.
You force the glass
across your wrist
as your skin slits open
and rivers of blood
begin pouring out,
forming an ocean.
Your mouth parts open
in a helpless cry,
as you look
for your reflection

in the mirror.
Seeing only a panel
of nothing
as you crumble
onto the floor
into a heap,
becoming a nothing.

Prisoner of Your Mind

Paranoia -
those terrifying thoughts
that plague your mind.
Your body
is overwhelmed
by something heavy and hard
and blackness is all around you.
You try to escape,
but the blackness
is heavy with nightmares.
You force yourself
to seek for some light,
but it keeps on weaseling,
pushing, sneaking,
and thrusting it's way in,
pushing your sanity away -
far, far away and out of touch.
You try to take action,
but your mind
refuses to give your body
the opportunity to do so.
You are stuck
in your body,

so stiff and rigid,

as your mind

goes a thousand miles an hour.

And your last

sane thought

is that you are

a prisoner of your mind.

OK To Be a Human

Falling

F
A
L
L
I
N
G

F
A
L
L
I
N
G

into a dark pit.

There's no end,

no floor,

and no hands to catch me.

T H U M P!

I fall on the bottom

of the pit.

All I see is darkness.

There's no hope,

no escape,

and nothing that

is worth praying for.

Time

is now my greatest enemy.

I gotta get out

before the trap is sprung.

I run around

like a chicken with it's head cut off.

All the materials

and knowledge in my head

is pretty useless.

My voice box

is at it's top volume.

After a while,

time used up so much of my energy,

and my voice

began to waver

until it's down

to the dial

that spells MUTE.

My hands

began clawing the walls

like a wild animal.

The salt water tears

began coursing down my cheeks.

Ashamed of my tears,

I hastily wiped them off,

refusing to admit my defeat.

My pride is

too important to me.

I choked back

my emotions,

willing myself to become a stone.

Now I am

the mountain.

I seethe with rage.

My fists

were clenching into tight balls.

My eyes

were blazing

with fury.

And I turned up the volume

of my voice box,

screaming as if

I have never screamed before.

And the mountain

began to rumble

and then it crumbled

onto the ground into a heap.

My screams turned

into sobs.

All were lost

as the sea of my tears

drowned me.

The water level

began raising

until there was a light.

I reach out

for some contact

and suddenly, I'm safe.

I was pulled

out of the pit.

And I realized

that it was ok

to be a human sometimes.

The Box

There was this box
that everyone adored.
Everyone, except for me
for I could not understand
what the box provided
or what it meant.
I could not figure out
what everyone saw in it.
People were swaying,
having a good time.
As I stood there
like a dummy,
feeling left out
and blind to the box.
I reached out
and laid my hand
on the box.
Vibration shot through
my body like an electric current,
and my head
began developing beats
connected to the box.
I started to dance,

moving with the beats,

my hand still on the box.

It felt good

for a while

and the box

advanced itself to a radio.

I was a part

of their world...

or so, I thought.

And then,

I wanted more.

I wanted to know

what the radio was saying,

what it sounded like.

I wanted to get

in touch with the emotions

of the songs.

I wanted

what everyone else had.

I strained,

hoping to hear something.

But the radio

continued to boom,

separating me from everyone else

and I was

forced to deal with the fact

that I was Deaf.

I struggled

to be a part

of their world.

But the radio

continued to push me away.

I picked up the radio

and held it against my chest,

letting myself feel high

with the beats,

savoring what I could have.

As my anger grew

stronger and stronger

and the radio

reduced itself to a box.

I flung it

against the wall,

smashing the box

into pieces.

And the room stopped moving.

I walked over to it,

and laid my hand on it.

It was still...

and identical to my world.

That Last Night

That last night...

the one I remember so clearly.

It was dark and cold

outside the window.

The night sky was black

and filled with diamond-like stars.

The window

was covered with frost.

I stood there,

shivering

inside a warm room.

A figure was laying on a bed;

my father's mother.

The woman who I lived with

for years.

The one who I bickered with,

played pranks on, and tagged along with.

The woman who I loved

to aggravate

was now helpless,

and there was nothing

I could do

to help her.

I turned to the frost-covered window

and looked up toward the sky.

And my finger

traced out the words on the window;

"Watch over my grandmother."

As soon as I was done writing,

the words were suddenly replaced

with frost.

What an icy request

I had made.

I gave her a kiss,

and went on home,

keeping my eyes on the sky.

And two weeks later,

after being transferred to a nursing home,

she was gone.

During those last two weeks

of her life,

did I go to visit her?

Did we get to say good bye?

And most of all;

did she know

that I really loved her?

And now,

all I could think of

was what it would be like

if she was still alive,
and if I would have
treated her differently.
But like that last night,
there was nothing I could do
but to remember
that she was my grandmother
and I love her.

Found Out!

Getting high
in a world
with friends.
In the basement,
where we puffed away.
Giggling,
we stumbled up the stairs
and to the TV we went.
Snow White...
such a beautiful movie.
The colors
were so vivid,
yet so real.
We were flying
through our world
until
THEY went downstairs.
Our world
was still there,
yet we panic.
I thought
my life would end that night.
And THEY came back up.

We were all really tense.
Daddy's friend
finally gave us a knowing smile,
saying, "Why'd you smoke downstairs?"
Mom's friend
simply stood there,
giggling.
We fought so hard
to keep our eyes on the movie.
And THEY came.
My parents,
working together as if I have never
seen them that way before.
They whispered,
leaned over to look at us,
and they went whispering again.
My mind,
mixed with both the real and "my world"
struggled for stability.
Tension was overpowering the room.
Finally our friends
stood up to leave,
trying very hard not to laugh.
I realized
my life was getting
closer and closer to the end.

They finally left.
My friend hastily
stood up to escape
to the safety of my room.
I followed,
desperately wanting
to escape too.
But, to our luck,
my parents showed
up at my room TOGETHER.
We merely stared
at each other.
Finally Daddy said;
"I know."
I fumbled,
and mumbled,
and stammered,
trying to proclaim our innocence.
My Mom,
as naive as she was,
started defending me,
"It was nothing. It was a cigarette,"
she said.
Daddy continued to shake
his head no.
Finally I sighed.

"Daddy," I said
"Do you want me
to tell you the truth,
or shall I lie?"
He stared at me
in the eyes.
"Truth," he answered.
I stared right back
at him.
"You're right, Daddy,"
I said.
"Are you mad?"
My mom
practically went into shock.
My Daddy then,
smiled.
No.

Running

I am confused...
Here I am
at a crossroad.
Nowhere to run,
nor anyone to turn to.
There were too many
deaf ears
and eyes that are blind.
The world is moving.
Everyone has got their places.
All, except for me,
so I keep on running
to continue moving.

Running, running
with no sense of direction
or any goal.
My mind is on overload,
yet I can not make any sense of
nor keep track of my mind.
I am merely running;
running deaf and blind
Not knowing whether

I am coming or going.
I do care, I do want
to know where I am going,
but all I can do is run.

Running, running
My legs are getting too tired
to run any more...

Grandma Ruth

I have known you
for twelve years.
My earliest memory of you
was you babysitting me
at your apartment.
I remember how
you went out of your way
to make sure I was comfortable...
I miss you, Grandma Ruth.

I remember all those visits
to your apartment on South Washington Street.
I remember your kitchen, all yellow and white,
and your pink and white bathroom
with a soft toilet seat cover.
And I definitely remember
the last room with a big piano in your apartment
which I thought was haunted...
I miss you, Grandma Ruth.

I remember chasing
your little black cat, Tootsie.
I remember
your Camel cigarettes, your crossword puzzles,

and your games of solitaire.
I remember
your dog, Duke
and your big, old fashioned desk...
I miss you, Grandma Ruth.

When I was seven,
you moved in to live with us,
along with your oh-not-so-little-anymore Tootsie.
We were neighbors
as my bedroom was next to yours.
We fought day and night
and I would play pranks on you
which would make you mad...
I miss you, Grandma Ruth.

I was mean to you
and you always said
I was a bold, spoiled kid.
Yet there were nights
when I would peek into your room
and you would invite me in with such love.
But one day,
you were gone...
I miss you, Grandma Ruth.

I think of you constantly
and I hope you know
how much I miss and love you.
I wish I spent more time with you
and got to know you better.
I wish I knew more
of my Jewish heritage and who I am.
I wish I could tell you how much I love you...
I miss you, Grandma Ruth.

I promise
I will carry on your memory
with pride and love.
You were one great woman
who was also very intelligent.
I hope I will be like you.
I am lucky
to be your granddaughter.
I love you, Grandma Ruth!

Peace

Peace.
What is peace?

The beautiful snow capped mountains
of Mt. Hood,
The beautiful, rhythmic waves
of the Pacific.
To me, that is peace.

The beautiful streets
with small shops in Seaside,
The scenic drive
along the coast.
To me, that is peace.

Eating by a beautiful view
of the Pacific,
Running across the sand
and dipping a toe in the ocean.
To me, that is peace.

The huge outdoor flea market
with all kind of stuff and people.

Riding the max
across the city of Portland.
To me, that is peace.
42

Oregon equalize peace,
and I shall go back one day.

To Dad, With Love

This is a big world, Dad,
filled with good and evil.
But I grew up safe, Dad,
and happy, because of you.

We shared many special times, Dad.
I remember cuddling with you
in your chair, Dad,
and we laughed and talked with love.

You were so good to me, Dad.
You gave me everything in this world.
You even gave me the world, Dad,
and you did it out of love.

You took me everywhere, Dad.
We had a lot of fun.
You also taught me a lot, Dad.
You taught me about life.

I grew up adoring you, Dad.
You were my world.
I could not live without you, Dad.

For you are everything to me.

Now, I am getting older, Dad.
Nothing have changed,
except that I love you even more, Dad,
and you definitely are my world.

So, here is from me to you, Dad.
Thank you so much for everything.
You are one wonderful person, Dad.
And I love you very much.

My Dear Friend

My dear friend,
you are the best friend
anyone could ever have.
You make me so high
that life is lovable to me.
When I am depressed,
you knew exactly what to do.

My dear friend,
even though
you are against the law,
I will not give you up.
One hit of you,
and my problems fades away.

My dear friend,
you take me
so high and away
into that wonderful place
where everything
is seen through
a wise child's eyes.

My dear friend,
when you were not available,
my mind and soul
scream out for you,
wanting and needed to be taken away
into that secure place
where I can be happy.

My dear friend,
the cops patrol around
in search for you.
People educate the others
on the dangers you bring.
And I ask why,
it's simple, they do not know you.

My dear friend,
you have been smuggled,
sold, traded for, stolen,
fought over and killed for
by people everywhere
as you are valued,
and we love you.

My dear friend,
all I care about
is how good
you are to me,
and I love you for that.
You are my dear friend.

Why?

You lied.
You cheated.
You conned.
You manipulated.
But I still
think the world of you.
Why?

You made promises
that were not always kept.
You said things
that were not always true.
But I still
think the world of you.
Why?

Sometimes I would spend
hours and hours
waiting for your call,
or for you to pick me up.
But I still
think the world of you.
Why?

Your words were

golden to me.

Your actions were heroic in my eyes,

no matter how immoral they may be.

But I still

think the world of you.

Why?

Why? I would like to know why!

Questions

Who really does care?
Who is honest?
Who can I trust?

There are too many
people around,
yet I feel so lonely.

I keep on running
away from everything
and everyone.

Life, to my eyes,
is one big mess,
and there seem to be no end.

My mind
struggles against me
and my body.

I feel myself
falling into a total darkness,
and it is unbearable.

What is life?

Who are people?

I honestly do not know.

51

All I know

is that

I am beginning not to care anymore.

Driving Across America

We got into the car,

and we drove,

and drove,

and drove.

We went to Pennsylvania first

to set affairs in order,

and to pack,

and to say "see you later."

We went to Ohio.

The night fell,

and there was nothing to see,

but rain, rain and rain.

We went to Indiana,

it was still dark.

But the rain

had finally let up.

We went to Illinois.

It was still night.

We talked and talked,

and we continued to drive.

We went to Missouri,
my uncle's home state.
We saw the arch
and a casino boat on the river.

We went to Oklahoma.
It was finally a sunny morning.
But we saw the site
of the Oklahoma City bombing.

We went to Texas.
It was sunny,
but all those cows
were not pretty to look at.

We went to New Mexico.
The desert was amazing!
It was so warm,
teasing us that California was nearby.

We went to Arizona.
The sun had beautifully set,
but then the rain began to pour.
The air pressure in my ears were deadly.

We finally arrived in California,

but my ears were killing me.

My headache was pounding,

and I nearly got run over by two rich bitches.

The next morning,

California was beautiful,

warm, sunny,

and held many exciting promises.

I look back now

It definitely was worth it!

I love California

And I loved the whole experience!

Bottle of Temptation

The bottle of temptation
sitting there in front of me.
It looks so innocent
and so delicious.
My mind
started a war with itself.
During the war,
the bottle sits there,
not having a care in the world,
while my mind
and my health
are at risk.
I decided to take the plunge
and I say; "only one."
I take a sip
and suddenly I'm in heaven.
The bottles seem to keep
on lining up for me
as I try to take in
as much as possible.
And soon I wake up
with an ugly hangover
and a failed memory of the night before.
For each weekend,

the story continues.
Until one weekend
turned into a disaster.
I woke up in a hospital bed
with blood all over myself.
I saw myself hooked up
to a heart monitor,
an IV tube stuck in me,
and a lacerated lip.
And I thought;
it's all over...
I'm in trouble...
In trouble I am!
All because of this dumb bottle -
the bottle of temptation -
called alcohol.

Lost Without the Light

The world is dark
without the promise
of the light,
leaving me
with feelings
of hopelessness.
I am lost.

The light has
gone from my world.
I wanted
to disappear
just like the light did,
so that it would not hurt as much.
I am lost.

Bumping,
Scratching,
Scraping,
Falling,
Bruising,
Hurting myself in the dark,
I am lost.

I need the light back,
so that my world
would be visible once again.
I want to smile
into the mirror,
and have it smile back.
I am lost.

I am counting
the minutes,
and hoping
I will have
the beauty of the light
back into my world soon,
so I would not be lost anymore.

What Happened? And Why?

When someone said
love is tough...
That person certainly
knew what he/she was talking about.

When we first
got together
almost seven months ago,
you were sure of us.

We went through a lot
together,
and I thought
you loved me as much as I loved you.

I have asked you
countless of times
if you were sure of us,
and if you still wanted to be with me.

And each times,
you would say yes.
Yes, you were sure of us.

Yes, you still wanted to be with me.

I believed you.
I allowed myself to love you fully.
I devoted my life to you.
I believed in us.

Now, all that had changed.
I am so lost.
For you were my life,
and you no longer are.

How do I deal with you?
How was I supposed to act?
What was I supposed to say?
What should I do now?

My heart had been ripped out.
My emotions are all screwed up.
I have never felt so lost before.
I am so, very hurt.

While you stand there
with a smile on your face.
"Hey girl, what's up, my friend?"
You say it so casually.

How could you?

Why did you hurt me this way?

Why are you doing this?

What do you want?

Help me, please.

You got me into this

Now I need some answers

But one thing...

I really did love you

And you abused it.

What happened?

And why?

Our Ties

When we first met,
our ties were
quickly connected
and tightened.

Over a period of time,
our ties were
intertwined with each other,
and we were very close.

Then one day
you decided to
cut our ties
and we were apart.

I was lost,
my string lagging
along behind me
with no end.

But we still
had another kind
of tie called
friendship.

Still something
seems to be wrong.
Our tie is very loose,
and I am scared.

I hope
you will not
severe the only tie
we have left.

We came into this
with strong ties.
Let's not come out
of this with nothing.

Fuck Off

Fuck you.
Fuck you.
Fuck you.
Fuck you, bitch.

Fuck you
for hurting me.
You know it,
but you still hurt me anyway.

Fuck you
for throwing insults at me,
which tore me apart,
and for your insensitivity.

Fuck you
for expecting me
to smile and
forgive you right away.

Fuck you.
I am not a toy.
I am a human being.
So, fuck off.

My Lifesaver

People see you
and they go
"What a beautiful cat."

But to me,
you are more than a cat.
You are a lifesaver.

I embraced death
with a noose around my neck
and bloody wrists and knife.

I was ready
to leave this world
with such hatred.

The noose around my neck
was getting tighter.
The blood continued to flow from my wrists.

But then you came up to me,
and looked at me
with eyes filled with love.

You brought back
feelings of
life, love, and hope.

You sat by me
with a beautiful innocence
and filled me with guilt.

Slowly the rope
was released,
and the knife dropped onto the floor.

I sank down on the floor
and took you into my arms,
crying for life.

You are not
merely a cat,
but a lifesaver.

They Know… Everyone Know…

Walking into a
brightly lit supermarket,
feeling all those eyes on me.

They know... everyone know...

My eyes dart
around the store with shame.
Feeling self conscious, I walk.

They know... everyone know...

Toward the freezer section,
my pace increasing
with every step I took.

They know... everyone know...

Pretty soon, I am flying.
Aisles by aisles went by
until everything became a blur.

They know... everyone know...

I took a reality check.
I am running,
and attracting attention.

They know... everyone know...

With an internal groan,
I slide to a stop.
Act normal! I tell myself.

They know. Everyone know...

Peering over my shoulder, I grab
the first vanilla ice cream I see
as if I was a hardened criminal.

They know... everyone know...

With my precious ice cream,
I race to the cashier.
It's halfway over, I remind myself.

They know... everyone know...

I practically thrust
my money in her hand,

and began to pray.

They know... everyone know...

Hurry up, lady! I silently beg,
as paranoia was starting
to overwhelm my whole being.

They know... everyone know...

Grabbing at my change
and my precious ice cream
I went through so much for.

They know... everyone know...

In a second, I was racing out
the doors and to my car,
my beloved ice cream in my hands.

They know... everyone know...

In my car, I sit with relief,
as I slowly began to realize I was being
unnecessarily overly paranoid.

They know... who knows???

My logical side takes over.
I would not have to experience this
if I would have just relaxed.

Who knows? And who cares?

I start to laugh.
All this just because I was stoned,
and I wanted ice cream.

Where Did She Go?

Raised by two
loving, adoring parents,
she was the only child
and everything
they wanted her to be,
and more...

Where did she go?

She had the beauty,
and also the brain.
She loved to read,
read, and read.
Everywhere she went, her books went.
Her parents were so proud!

Where did she go?

She had an overly
active imagination.
She put her creativity
into everything she did,
be it writing stories, poetry,
and losing herself into fantasy.

Where did she go?

She loved to be in
the center of attention.
She loved to be
a part of everything,
be it her family, her friends,
her school, and her community.

Where did she go?

Her parents loved her.
Her grandparents adored her.
Her teachers praised her.
Her friends admired her.
But most of all,
she loved herself.

Where did she go?

I sit here, weeping,
as I know of her whereabouts.
I had to love myself
in order to bring
us together,
and that was where she went.

One Comes After Another

I want to
be alone.
And to dress
all in black.
I want to
stay in a dark room
all day and sleep,
as I am miserable...

I want to
smoke weed
until I pass out.
I want to
use cocaine
until I overdose.
I want to
forget my existence...

I want to
get into my car
and drive until
I smash into something.
I want to

Slit my wrists
and watch my blood
fill the tub...

I want to
close my eyes
and sleep forever.
I want to
be nonexistent on earth.
I want to
be outside of my body.
I want to die...

Unfortunately
life and death
Does not fit together.
One comes after another.

Good Night

Immersed with each other
Through the hazy smoke
We sat and smoked
Our lives on journeys
Our emotions at peace

Suddenly the door
Flew open
The police were peering in
Holding up their badges
Keeping their noses covered

I thought I saw
My life die in front of my eyes
The worst possible scenario
Was unfolding in front of our eyes
We were helpless, totally helpless

Roaches were sprawled
Around us, in front of us
We were separated
By a hazy blanket of smoke
Our bodies frozen to the spot

"Get up" they commanded
We obeyed, for authority
We marched down the stairs
And were ordered
To sit on the floor

In stocking feet
We sat, vulnerable
And shivering with fear
No communication was possible
I had really done it this time

To my horror,
My best friend
Was being frisked by the police
I felt for her,
And I feared for myself

My turn came
There was nothing
I could do
I silently stood up,
Putting my hands on the wall

The police's hands
Were on my thighs
Sliding up toward my pocket
Where they crept inside

And lingered around

I stood, frozen on the spot
My body, all stiff
Yet shivering with deep fear
My head was spinning
I worried what would happen next

Her hands slid
Up my waist and then my torso
And she cupped
My breasts with her hands
"Damn the authorities," I thought

A lowly American citizen
Powerless to do anything,
Or to challenge the authority
I have accept my defeat
I was powerless

Merely a citizen, I was
My life in strangers' hands
My future at stake
All because of the damn weed
And the damn authorities

Before our minds
Had time to figure out

What the hell was going on,
The police gave us
Our other big shock

Their attention were turned elsewhere
A policeman looked at us
With a smile and a laugh
"You smoked. You're high,"
With a scolding finger

The whole thing was too much
Just too much
My best friend
Started to laugh hysterically
I was lost, very lost

All I knew was that
We had a real close call
What if we were
Not as lucky the next time?
It was not worth the risk

Yet I wonder about tonight
Was it all in our head?
I really had to double check
"No, it happened!" My best friend stated
Shit. This was too surreal

Too surreal
That we had such an experience
And that we got away free
All because they were busy
Arresting other people for a different crime

We were simply
In the wrong place
At the wrong time
Yet we got out
What a trip, I gotta call it a night

Good night
And yes,
It happened
And yes,
I am now really thinking

Good night

Thank You, My Crush

My world was so unclear
So blurry, and so confusing
I got swept away
In all the chaos

Getting online as usual
Your name seduced
My whole attention
With one click, we were in touch

Old feelings, old flashbacks
Rekindled my inner candle
I was glowing brightly
Fantasy became reality

With some unknown chemistry
You had waken up a part
In me which I thought of as
Dead, long gone, and impossible

Just from you alone
My world was finally
A-blazing with light
I feel so alive!

Thank you, my crush
For a beautiful wake up call
As the candle of mine
Is glowing so bright, at last!

On The Prowl

A steamy encounter
With a long-lost crush
My eyes, glued to the screen
And my fingers, to the keyboard
Typing, reading, and sharing
Hours flew by like seconds

I pant, like a love-struck teen
High sexual energy
Had me squirming in my seat
So aware of my sexuality, of my needs,
I go along, my desires being my priority
I am a wild animal, yearning to be freed

Wanting, desiring and craving
To get to know you more
In every ways imaginable
My arms, both outstretched,
Desperately grasping into thin air
As I will for my fantasy to become reality

Such a true representative
Of beauty and temptation you are,

Inspiring the leash on my neck
To come undone without any delay
And I find myself racing toward you
Letting my heart lead the way for once

The destination, in front of me,
Has not yet been revealed
But my heart is finally heard
Unleashed a wild beast
In me, you have done
As I am now on the prowl for reality

My Beautiful

Could it be true?

Is this for real?

We were told

About true love

We have heard

Fantastic love stories

We have searched,

Wished, hoped for, and dreamed

Of finding true love

We question

Whether true love exists

Now I stand

Gazing into your eyes

Your beautiful eyes

Your lips, your chin,

The way you laugh

The way you avert your head

To hide your shyness

The way you touched me

And how you held me

You are simply beautiful

Both inside and outside

The way my heart
Jumps at the sight of you
The way my skin tingles
When you touch me
The way my eyes light up
When I see you
The way I melt
When you kiss me
The way my heart stops
When I look at beautiful you
Is this too good to be true?

I sit here
In my bed
Gazing at your pictures
Flashbacks of you
Overwhelm my whole body
My mind, my soul, and my heart
Could it be true?
My beautiful
My heart is skipping joyously
I'm madly in love

With you, my beautiful
I am madly in love
Could it be true?

Is this for real?

I do not need

To ask

For my heart

Knows the answer,

My beautiful

I am madly in love

with you

True Love

I always thought
I had experienced
True love
Until I met you,
My beautiful
I was wrong,
Dead wrong

This thing
We have going on
Between us
Is so beautiful
So healthy
So wonderful
And so magical

I sit, crying
For I have found
What true love
Is all about
And I have you
To thank for that,
My beautiful

My first relationship
Never did amount
To the word "love"
Instead it was
Filled with hatred,
Jealousy, control
And abuse of all kind

Then you came
Into my life,
Bringing such beauty
To me, to life
To the word love
Especially the true meaning
Of true love

Because of you,
My beautiful,
I learned that
I deserve the very best
I deserve to love
And to be loved back
I deserve happiness

Thank you, my beautiful
For being a wonderful teacher
Thank you
For showing me

What true love is all about
Thank you for loving me
And allowing me to love you back

My beautiful,
You are truly
My true love
I love you,
My true love
And I will continue
To love you, my true love
I love you!

Fireworks

intense, electrifying passion
from deep within
quietly rumbling the ground
like fireworks being set off

shimmering, shining
heaving chests, spinning heads
flesh being flared to life
with a build up sound toward a loud bang

arms and legs setting off shadows
amongst the warm, rumpled pink sheets
mouths and tongues hungry and with intensity of love
danced as colorful fireworks exploded in the sky

It Is Who I Am

I was always
Daddy's little girl
I was even
Grandpa's little girl

Over the years
They would preach
Me about boys,
Telling me of their ways

They said that
Men were no good,
That they were
Out for just one thing

They said that
Men will not love me
For who I am,
But for my body

They would praise me
With delight and pride
On how smart I was

For remaining single

With a pat on my head
By those two men I adored the most,
I would beam with pride
And agree along happily

I am of a better class
Than those of the male species
I am way above
Those boys and those men

The more years
That went by,
The longer
I remained single

The longer I was single,
The more concerned
My father and grandpa
Were about the idea

"Who is your boyfriend?"
"How come you don't have one?"
They would often ask
I would always shrug

"Haven't met the right man."
"Didn't have time for men"
I would simply explain
Without any further thought

Yet deep inside
I always had
This nagging feeling
That it was not the case

I always knew
I was different
From my peers
And my family

For years, I struggled
With my secret,
Trying to live
In accordance to society

I tried to
Please my family
I tried to
Please society

Yet I knew
I would never
Be free or be happy
If I continued to lie

The older I got,
And with my experiences,
I came to a realization
That I love women

With women,
I can be myself,
Find happiness,
And enjoy life

Thinking back about
My father and my grandpa,
I find their preaching
Very ironic, yet funny

But I knew
They had nothing to do
With my identity
As it was who I am

It is who I am
It is my identity
I am a woman
And I love women

To hell with society
I am living
My life for myself
I have not been this happiest!

I am not going to let others
Decide on my identity for me
I am a lesbian
And I shall be proud

Not for my father or grandpa
And not for society
I will be who I am
And that is who I am

I am a proud lesbian
Madly in love with my true love
And it is time or the world
To know that it is who I am

Destiny

Thin, black veil
Enveloping the moon
With it's magic
And fate was she
Destiny was her name
Dancing with temptation
Flirting with Lady Mystery
The mask of seduction
Have she been uncovered
Wild ocean of passion
Intertwining with the calm air
For there a grand ballroom
In the night sky
And fate was she
Destiny was her name

Ocean of Life

The ocean
Just like life

The waves
Pulling us in
Pushing us away
Pulling us in again

Seducing us
Into loving life
Giving life meanings
Especially the beauty of living

Then it makes us
Hate life
Tempting us
Toward our death

The waves
Rolling in and out
Softly and tenderly
Harshly and deadly

Either we get washed ashore
Or we drown
In the end
It kills us

Life kills
Yet we swim

World of Silence

Watching her from afar
As my heart aches
To have and hold her
Yet I must restrain myself...

Wishing for time
To fast forward
So I can once again
Reunite with my true love...

Her beautiful smile,
Her movement, her walk,
Her words, her attention,
I want her all to myself...

Yet we must remain silent
Our eyes make contact
Cautiously and nervously
As if we were strangers...

While our eyes
Bled silently with love
And knowledge

That this was a world of silence...

Complete strangers
In the outside world,
Soulmates and true loves we are
In our own private world...

Oh, how I crave
To have those two worlds
Join and become one
And that would be heaven...

As she is mine,
All mine alone and no one else's
I want to show off
My Beautiful to the world...

Yet we must remain silent
Just like our repressed eyes
As this world, unfortunately,
Still believes in silence...

A Beautiful Combination

Pools of delicious chocolate
Filled with love and wisdom
Set deeply in that gaze
Drawing me in deeper and deeper...

A beautiful set of lips,
So inviting, so comforting
Which can kiss so good
Sending my mind into an overdrive...

A lovely smile
That goes on and on
Making me feel so high
Yet so special and adored...

Luscious, flowing hair
Of an extraordinary color
Setting off a golden halo,
Reflecting such goodness...

An attractive pair of hands
Which know how to comfort
Yet how to please

Sending me to stardom...

Strong, protective arms
That embrace me
With such tenderness and security
Allowing me to drown in them...

A warm, soft body
Filled with confidence and beauty
Engulfing me with passion
And sheltering us in our own world...

With a wise mind
Which lets out streams of words
Filled with wonderful things
That makes me feel so special...

And especially a big heart
So sensitive, and very caring
Which produced positive energy
Making me feel so loved...

All of this combination
Comes to this;
A beautiful person
No wonder I love you to infinity and back!

The Final Resting Place

Sitting by this
Freshly covered grave
The sky was black
Except for a full moon
Shedding light on the cemetery
Its' silverly-like threads filtering
Through the heavy wrought iron gates
Giving it a somber mood

Looking at all the flowers
Covering the fresh mound of dirt
Envisioning the scenery
That had taken place recently
The spiritual leader routinely
Doing the service
People mourning the one
They loved and lost

Wondering of this lost soul
That once was alive
Breathing, thinking, feeling,
A whole human being
Filled with warm blood

And a mind and soul
Roaming through life
With a place in society

Seeing an image
Of the corpse
Nestled in a coffin
Six feet under
All cold and embalmed
Getting ready to deteriorate
Becoming nonexistent on earth
With only a tombstone to mark its' life

Laying my hand on one headstone
Out of many, which littered
The cemetery, the home of the dead,
On the land of the living
As I sadly acknowledged the fact
That one day this moon-lit place
Will be more than just a cemetery
For it will be my final resting place

The Little Girl

A little girl,
Filled with innocence
All dressed up
In girlish clothes
With hair of curls
Held back by ribbons
And a smile so big
Trusting and loving the world

Daddy's little girl
Mommy's little playmate
Grandpa's favorite
Grandma's sweetheart
The beautiful child
With charm enough
To have people's hearts
Wrapped around her little finger

One day, she grew up
That little girl had gone somewhere
Knowledge and experiences
Had hardened her heart
Time had tired her

And slowed her down
People had screwed her over
One way or another

Loathed the world and people
Had she done and obsessed about,
Especially hatred for life
Her mouth, set in a downward position
Her eyes, low on the ground
Her head, bent over in avoidance
She came and went, here and there
With emotions, so scarred and messed up

Until she was blessed
With the permanent present and beauty
Of true love in her life
Struggled against the goodness she did
For negativity and depression were habits
She soared, crashed, and soared again
With the love, patience and support
Given unconditionally by her true love

Her mouth smiling, her eyes twinkling,
Her head high, her body proud,
A swirl of beauty, happiness, life, and love
Went with her wherever she went

Death was finally so far away,

As her true love had opened her eyes

To a beautiful side of life,

Especially the little girl within

Entrapped

Life is wonderful
Love is beautiful
Yet why am
I so dark inside?

I cry out for help
It is like
No one could hear
Even though they try to listen

Torrid, stormy seas
Sweep into my mind
My soul screams out
To be freed from my body

Thunder and lightning
Battle out inside me
While the outside held
Roses, wines and sunshine

I am entrapped
Inside my own mind
And my own body

I am my own prisoner!

Searching for ways
To get rid of all this
I struggle to see clearly
Through my flooded tears

Life is beautiful
Love is wonderful
Still I need help
As I am entrapped

Day and Night

As known,
Day and night
Are exactly the opposite
Yet I still love you
Just the same
Throughout the day and at night

In the day,
Your face is masked
With cheerful animation
Not to mention
The love and adoration
I see in your eyes

At night,
With soft light streaming
Through the drawn blinds
Your eyes are closed
To your own world
Yet I still see the love there

In the day,
You are just as beautiful
Not to mention your embraces,

Your warm laughters, your sun-winning smiles
You bury me with love
Bringing rainbows to each days

At night,
Your body besides me
Bringing warmth to me
Breathing love each second
As I kiss the tip
Of your nose with love

The beauty of all this
Is that your love
Remains just as strong
Throughout the day and at night
As well as I love you forever
Into millions of days and nights

Who Are You?

Who are you?
Who are you?
I asked questions
Yet I do not know
The answers

Who are you?
A beautiful woman
Very smart, very charming
So talented, so interesting
They answered

Who are you?
A cold-hearted bitch
Going nowhere in life
Very depressed, very obsessed
They answered

Who are you?
A loving person
Very helpful, very kind
A good listener, an empath
They answered

Who are you?
A whacked out psycho
With unstable emotions
And a scarred body
They answered

Who are you?
I silently plead
Looking into a mirror
Into a face staring back
Who are you?

The Question

Is there a God?
Some say He exists
Some say He does not
Some say He's the Heavily Father
Some say He's the Greater Spirit

Is there a God?
Or is there not a God?
I wonder almost everyday
Either using His name in vain
Or basking in my guilt about Him

If there is a God
Then where was He
When I was in need of help?
When I was very depressed?
When I was all alone?

If there is not a God
Then why do people
Waste their time
With all this mumbo jumbo,
Imposing guilt on others?

If there is a God
Then why do we have to suffer
Through this place we call Earth?
Why do we get born
And why do we die?

If there is not a God
Then what is the purpose of life?
Why do I hurt so much?
Why am I so lost?
Why do I exist?

Is there a God
This seems to be like an eternal question
With answers that would never
Be satisfying enough
So help me, what do I do?

A Wild Ride

Driving around
In a seedy part of the city
Wanting and needing
To satisfy my craving
A fix is what I desire for
As my eyes roam around
For a potential drug fiend
Shooting glances over my shoulder
For any sign of cops
My hands sweating on the steering wheel

A man wobbles around
Waving us down, motioning for us to come
Desperation filled my very soul
As I slowed down and stopped by him
"Rock?" He asked, "Rock?"
I shook my head no, "weed"
"No have weed," he stated
My heart slowly sank to my stomach
Before I knew it, he called out to his woman
And they both hopped into my car

They motioned for me to take them
As they will take us to weed
Laughter bubbled up and died in my throat
When I realized how far I was going
By taking two complete strangers on a ride
With their eyes, all reddened and drugged,
And the smell of alcohol filling my car
I drove on, following directions,
Stopping in the middle of a street
Whereas they took our money and left

We sat, like pathetic fools we were,
And waited for nearly an hour
Visions of being stoned danced in our head
Yet our stomach fluttered anxiously
For those strangers to reappear
Sunset gave away light to darkness
As the moon shone brighter and brighter
Our hopes faded away and away
For we knew our money we will never see again
Especially our chance of being stoned were taken away

An ugly and dark rage came over me
And we finally spotted them lingering around
I angrily confronted them up close and personally
Their drugged eyes were glazed over

From the drinks they probably enjoyed with our money
They nervously avoided my every move
With a disgusted groan, I turned away
And back to my car, spinning dirt with my tires
As we sped away, from this heavily drugged scene
Taking with us a memory of this wild ride

It Wins, Again!

Obsessing

Dwelling

Haunting

Taunting

Over and over

Again and again

Same thing

One certain thing

One particular thing

Weed

Marijuana

Mary Jane

Cannabis

Roaches

Joints

Blunts

Pipes

Bongs

My eyes, staring

My fingers, itching

My nose, twitching

My lips, licking
My mouth, watering
My throat, craving
My esophagus, anxious
My lungs, waiting
My head, eager

To see
To touch
To roll
To hold
To smell
To taste
To inhale
To exhale
To fly

Oh, sheer torture!
My obsessive mind
Is playing a game with me
My body system,
Crying out withdrawal!
For goodness's sake,
Just go to the damn weed
And get it lit up
For it wins, again!

A Dainty Little Fairy

If only I was
A dainty little fairy,
Twittering amongst the mildew filled grasses
On the ground, deep in the forest,
Where the owls hoot, and the birds sing
I will flutter around in my dainty little slippers
And my glittery wings of pretty colors

If only I was
A dainty little fairy,
Hovering near where people are
Watching over them, with motherly love
In my little pretty bucket, I will carry
Magic glitters of love, fortune, and happiness
Sprinkling them here and there, where needed

If only I was
A dainty little fairy,
My head, with a crown of wild flowers
My dress, spread out above my knees
And a pretty bodice, holding my busts up
Spreading around an air of feminism
Letting my beauty spill all over earth

If only I was

A dainty little fairy,

Holding hands with my beautiful fairy

We shall dance all over the world

Infesting everyone with love

For we have plenty of it to go around

As we want everyone on in their fairylands

Under the Spell

In the darkness
Of the night
The black light
Illuminating the view,
Creating an illusion
As the eyes locked on mine
With such intensity
The teeth, baring
And dripping with lust
The mouth, open
And swollen with passion,
Closing in onto my lips
As the two bodies
Latched together in ecstasy,
Bringing heaven down
Faster and faster
Until we are
Swept away flying
Through an underground world
As the mouth of yours
Sucks the life out of me,
Making two into one
And I surrender all my being

To you, my beautiful vampire,

For I am under

Your spell once again...

The Day at a Bookstore

Months and months, years after years
Books and magazines went by the cashiers
As the cash registers smoothly rang
And the drawer opened with a clang
I made my purchases with a smile
And walked out of the store in style

Until one day, I had courageously laid down
A lesbian magazines, it's cover faced down
Along with other books I wanted to buy
Suddenly my confidence went awry
When the magazine would not scan
And the voice of that uncultured salesman

Boomed on the loudspeaker, for all to hear
"Price for the lesbian magazine?" His lips, so clear
Quickly the heads turned, and the eyes peered at me
As if I was some kind of display, for all to see
I quickly smiled, holding my head up with pride
For I am a lesbian and nobody will make me hide

No such ignorance of the people will change me
Nor will they, or the society, make me want to flee

I am a true woman, and I shall be free
I took my purchases and left the store with glee
Putting ignorance and discrimination to shame
For my true self and my identity, I had chosen to claim

Glinting Piece of Metal

Sharp, sleek, smooth
Words I would use
To describe this
Glinting piece of metal

An useful tool
Yet a deadly weapon
This razor lays ahead
In front of my eyes

It's blade silently
Screaming out to me
To slice through
And cutting up skin

My head conjures up
An image of my body
So many tempting places
Yet wisely chosen, it must be

A thought of the razor
Ripping through my arm
Sends delicious sensations

Throughout my whole body

The idea of blood
Heavy, dark, and dripping
Gushing through the open wound
Deepens the temptation even more

The feeling of pain,
Bringing me in touch with my emotions
Forgetting the rage inside me
As I focus all my energy on the pain

Yet one little mistake
Can cost me so much
Such as hospitalization
Or even worse, death

I stare at it with lust
All the power it held
Was so fascinating
Yet I must be careful

For this single
Glinting piece of metal
Can decide on my fate
Which could be worse than death

My hand close around it

As I once again

Used the razor

To shave my legs

Another Day Still Goes By...

Nobody understand
How much I really hurt
Nobody could ever know
How I really feel

All this tears
That I am shedding
Are tears of
Anger, pain, rage, and sadness

It seems like
No matter how much I cry,
My tears are all useless
As another day still goes by

My chest is bursting
With heavy, bad feelings
My skin is tingling
For razors to be used on it

My anger is scary
As it is really dangerous
It makes me want to

Cry, hit, hurt and scream

Yet I am stuck
Instead my wretched temple
My body, restraining
My soul from being let out

And the war goes on
With my mind and my soul
On the opposite sides
As another day still goes by...

Poisoned!

The floor swayed
And the room began to spin,
For you have poisoned
My heart with love
And the poison had crept
Into my blood,
Coursing throughout
My body
Until my heart beat
Began pumping out
Your name
My love
My love
My love
Until it became
My necessity,
And it became
My life
As my heart beats
To a beautiful music of
True love
Such is music, such is life
Especially true love
For
I have been
Poisoned!

The Grim Reaper

Walking up to this
Heavy wrought iron gates,

The wind had suddenly
Started blowing up a gust

And the chilly air pierced me
Deep down to my bones

Grabbing the iron bars
With my gloved hands,

I nestled my head
Between the bars of the gate,

Staring out at rows and rows
Of tombstones and of mausoleums

Which filled the cemetery
With flowers littering the lawn,

Over many and many graves
All of those lives, once lived

Now lost out to the world
Of the utter unknown

A curtain of loneliness swirled around,
Giving the cemetery an eerie mood,

Beckoning anyone to join, if they dared
For after all journeys on Earth,

The Grim Reaper shall appear
The cemetery stood, finally taunting

For when we turn away
From the heavy wrought iron gates,

The Grim Reaper will still find us
Someday, and somehow

Let Me Call You Sweetheart

Let me call you sweetheart

Forever yours, as said my heart

For in this complicated world

And with all of life's burdens,

When everything was dreadfully dark

And what I had left in me was no more than a spark

Then you came along, with your beautiful smile,

Making fantasy reality,

and how I drove hundreds of miles

Finally reunited we were,

and the sun came up the next morning

You gave me no reason to go back into mourning

Let me call you sweetheart

Forever yours, as said my heart

Months flew off the calendar and days turned in over a year

Memories grew and expanded, and upward and onward, they did veer

Making me smile, of such incidents, like the tag in front of your t-shirt

And at a Hard Rock Cafe in Atlanta, how we flirted well beyond dessert

And such trips to Destin, Florida and Lake Erie we had gone
on

Stopping at various spots, bringing fog to the windows of our
car, well into dawn

Until we had exhausted ourselves physically, but never did we
tire of each other

For there is nowhere else I want to be, for you are the one and
there is no another

Let me call you sweetheart

Forever yours, as said my heart

My heart beats for you, only you

My life is you, and it can not be undone

As you are my future, which is filled with sunshine

I am as much of yours as you are of mine

And together, we shall create rainbows as if there was no
tomorrow

Making happiness infinity as if there was no sorrow

So, my beautiful, will you take my hand and let me call you
sweetheart

For you, my valentine, is the reason for the beating of my heart

Let me call you sweetheart

Forever yours as said my heart

Me A Woman!

With the swing of my hips
And a smile on the corner of my lips,
I bat my baby blue eyes slowly
Watching men grovel, as they are lowly
All just because I am a woman, a proud one
And men need us just like how plants need the sun

With the curves of my breasts,
Every womanhood's best
And in my skin, I comfortably fit
I am a woman and loving it
Proud of my sexuality, I am
Call me missus, call me ma'am

Where Are You, Pap?

Where are you?
You used to be so full of life
Smiling, teasing, and hugging
All those times you and I spent
Snuggling together on your lazy chair
Writing poems and solving word puzzles

And now you lay there
Barely covered by a sheet
In a skimpy hospital gown
With tubes going in and out of your body
And the machines beeping, and the IV tube dripping
In a dark, glass-covered room

Where are you?
You come in and out of consciousness
Drinking liquid with help,
to quench your thirst
With hands and feet tied down to the bed
"Who are you? I don't remember you," you say

I stood there, smiling bravely
As my heart was breaking

You may be there in a physical form
Yet, your mind has gone far away
Where have you gone? I wonder
I stood, like a stranger, in the room

Where are you?
Where have you gone?
Will you come back?
Will you ever recognize me again?
I long for you to once more say
"This is my favorite spoiled brat"

A World War II pilot,
A Penn State University graduate
A farmer, a high school teacher,
A brother, an uncle,
A husband, a father,
And a doting grandfather

You have played a big part in my life
A poet, you have turned me into
Also a lover of words and education
Alzheimer's disease may have taken you away
Yet forever, you will remain in my heart
And that is where you are, Pap

Searching for Home

Wandering around the place
In sweatpants that barely stayed on
Speaking nonsense with some glimmer of reality
As milk dribbled on the chin

The eyes, empty and without a soul
Words bitterly spoken and dripping with sarcasm
Head hung low, feet shuffling on the floor
Moving amongst people restlessly

I silently seated you down by me
And asked whether you recognized me
You answered "yes" with a sneer
"My mind is OK, but my heart is not"

So angry, yet so lost you were
For a man I deeply loved and cherished
Has gone and disappeared somewhere
Leaving behind a scary ghost of a stranger

I silently followed you around
With a heavy burden on my heart
For I can't seem to find you

And reality had struck me in the face

"Good bye" I sadly said with a hug
And you reached for your coat
"I don't know where home is," you said
Piercing my heart with arrows

How I hated having to go,
Leaving you behind in that nursing home
Yet sooner or later,
You will find your way home...

Utterly Impossible

Opening the door
To a funeral home
The face of my grandfather
Came into my view right away
All tucked away by a wall
Inside a black-silver coffin

Impossible... utterly impossible...

I approach slowly,
The flowers were flowing around
And on the top of the open coffin
As my grandfather's eyes
Were eternally closed in peace
With his hand atop one another

Impossible... utterly impossible...

His wedding band gleamed,
Tying him to his wife forever
I gaze at my grandfather
In a dark suit with a white shirt
And a blue and red diagonally striped tie,
His head nestled on a pillow

Impossible... utterly impossible...

People flowed in and out, paying their respect
As family members sobbed and hugged,
Talking amongst themselves quietly
As my grandfather laid there
In his coffin, oblivious to the world
For his soul has long gone

Impossible... utterly impossible...

After a prayer service,
We lined up to see him for the last time
Touching him, kissing him,
And whispering some words of love and prayers
As the blanket came above his waist
And was tucked under his chin

Impossible... utterly impossible...

The coffin was closed for the last time
And packed into a hearse by a group of men
As we started a slow, short procession
To the cemetery, his final resting place,
My eyes following the hearse in a daze
His last ride in a vehicle, down that road

Impossible... utterly impossible...

The grave was already dug, six feet deep
Awaiting for its' new resident
His body, merely an empty shell,
Never to be seen again by any of us
As the American flag, honoring him,
Was folded and handed to his wife of fifty five years

Impossible... utterly impossible...

An hour later his coffin was sheltered by earth
With flowers covering the fresh grave
I stood there, blinded with grief,
As memories flooded my head
And my heart ached with loss and sorrow
I had really lost my grandfather physically

Impossible... utterly impossible...

Another War

The world is all screwed up
No persons can be trusted
Wars are raging all over earth
For freedom and for lives

And you, with your closed mind
Are igniting a different kind of war
A war against your daughter
Her life, and her happiness

People are dying every day
Be it from the war, or homicide,
Or any sickness performed by
People upon another people

You are a part of that,
For killing your relationship
With your daughter,
For you could not approve of her lifestyle

Heroes and victims are recognized
With respect and acceptance
People of all kind, all races,

Sexual orientation, and religion

Yet I, your daughter's lover, do not exist in your eyes
No matter what goodness I do and did,
Your selfishness is blinding you,
And destroying you and your daughter

People are fighting everyday
As they will not give up
No matter what the cost is
They will fight to their death for their rights

And we are one of those people
For we are not going to lose
To oppression and to discrimination
We are fighting for our lives

So either you end the war
And both sides could be in peace
Or you can fight every day of your life
Until you destroy only yourself

Just Because

Just because I enjoy
Having full breasts in my hands
Caressing and stroking, nibbling and kissing

Instead of looking at a flat chest
Entangled with sweaty, matted hair
So undesirable, so revolting, so ugly

Just because I would rather lay my body over hers
Cupping a sweet, scented bottom with passion
My eyes, deep in hers, with love and promises

Instead of feeling the hardness
Of an ugly, wrinkly stick poking at me
As a disgustingly lowly pair of hands grope at me

Just because I enjoy caressing skin, so soft
Run my hands over the curves and the lines,
All the secrets within the body of a woman

Instead of torturing myself unhappily
Being in solitary company of a man,
Worrying what his next move might be

Just because I love to trace,

Kiss, taste and touch a warm, female face

And to run my fingers through her silky hair

Instead of standing stiffly and uncomfortable

With a Barbie-like smile on my face

As his rough chin brushes against my cheek

Just because society does not approve

Of me, as a woman, loving another woman

Does not mean I had to suffer

Instead I answer to the call of my heart,

Following it with such joy and love

As I live happily with my female lover

False Illuminations

The lips, closed
And curled up into a smile,
Giving out an image
Of a friendly face

But once
The lips separate,
Rows of pearly whites
Erupt into fangs

The hand,
Being offered
For a shake of friendship,
Or for support

With another hand
Behind the back
Holding a grisly,
Bloody knife

The eyes, smiling
And filled with sensitivity
As they bore into you,

Encouraging you to spill

As the mind is reeling,
Absorbing, and working,
Using whatever information it gets
Against you

False illuminations of friendship
Is something very unpleasant
You need to watch out for
Especially after your own back

Otherwise you will be destroyed
By the deception
Of good people, and of friendships
For those are false illuminations

Masks

People walk around
In masks every day
Claiming to be a friend
While they are out for only themselves

Except for a very few
Who dare to be true,
Wearing nothing but
Their real faces

Friends swarming on you
Like nasty mosquitoes
Taking, taking, and taking
Until your energy is drained

And you are on the floor
Bleeding and dying
As people scurry around,
Taking what they want

Only a very few true friends
Will stop and help you
And nurse you back to health,

Feeding you with their energy

And you are all whole again
Yet beaten, scarred, and tired
But older, wiser, and experienced
For you now know better

Liar, Liar

Liar, liar, pants on fire
As of your lies I tire
For honesty is the best policy
Yet with your conscience, so icy
Hell is going to freeze over
Before you screw me over

Liar, liar, pants on fire
It will all backfire
One way or another
I do not think your mother
Raised you this way
So away, you need to stay

Liar, liar, pants on fire
You need to join the choir,
Sing the praise of goodness
And ask for forgiveness
For your pants are on fire
Unless you want to expire

I Need a Nap

I waited and waited, Pap
Life is really too hard, I need a nap
I thought you loved me
I thought you would pick me up

I stood by the bus stop
With stormy weather pounding on me
I waited and waited, Pap
But the bus never came

I stood in the middle of the road
Everyone are screeching to avoid me
I waited and waited, Pap
But I did not get hit

I pressed the knife heavily down
On my wrists, waiting for the first trace of blood
I waited and waited, Pap
But I did not bleed to death

I laid my heart out on the table
And now it is filled with swords
I waited and waited, Pap

But I did not get sliced to death

I envisioned you in my head
Coming to take me with you
I waited and waited, Pap
I really need a nap

In Sync

Empty space gaining access
From the outside to the inside
It's heavy paned glass
Protecting the inside from the outside

Yet the image blurs
With rivers of raindrops
Running down the glass
Some went so far, some stopped shortly

Some made contact with the others,
Merging the rivers into streams into lakes
Some fell alone and slowly
With the pain of a breaking heart

My arm raised
To let my hand wipe away
The raindrops
For everything was so blurry

Only to discover it was also my eyes
Not only the clouds
That were leaking water
Human and nature are now in sync

Lady In Black

Driving angrily on the road
As a lady all in black
Grabbed my entire attention
With her thumb stuck out

A hitchhiker? I thought curiously,
Slowing down to take a good look
Then our eyes connected and held
A surge of hope came over her

She excitedly started toward me
Her eyes, filled with desperation
My pulse picked up its' pace
Yet I had no heart to turn her away

Smiling, I unlocked my Jeep
And she hopped right in
My name is Sarah, she says
I need to get to that town

I nodded and started driving
As my head filled up with thoughts
What if she had a weapon?

What if I became a victim?

She busied herself with her purse,
Fixing her face with make up
Her hair was in all direction
As I struggled to keep my breathing calm

We rode on in silence
For a few minutes
My paranoia, increasing
With every mile I drove

Finally we got to a red light
"Right here," she said, "thank you"
And she hopped out of my Jeep
As I stared after her in a daze

My anger was all forgotten
For it was replaced with danger
I murmured thanks for my safety
And wondered of this lady in black

The Coffee Mug

Countless of mornings at Grams and Pap's
With coffee by Pap's side, I would sit by his lap
And watched as his slender hand held the mug,
Bringing it to his lips now and then for a chug

Whenever my grandparents entertained company,
Out would come the coffee mugs, which tea would also
accompany
Aunts gossiped and uncles chatted through numerous of cups
Standing up now and then to get their mugs filled up

On some days, when I had gotten so sick,
Pap would bring me soup in the coffee mug so quick
And nursed me back to health in no time
With lots of love, making my illness a pastime

Time went by, and Heaven had claimed my Pap,
Leaving in our hearts a huge, missing gap
Grams came over with a box to my place
And my heart and soul, I needed to brace

For those coffee mugs belong to me now
And with each sip I took, Pap was with me, I know
For my days were started with a big smile,
Gearing me up for life filled with triumphs and trials

Closed For the Night

I wanted to go to the cemetery, but
It's so dark outside, and the sounds cried out
Erratically from deep down within me
For the sun has gone down
And the gates were sealed, closed
For the night
Rows of tombstones shone
Luminously under the eerie glow
Of the unsleeping moon
As the trees clawed menacingly
With images of ratty skeletons
Hidden amongst the ruthless shadows
And the ghosts laughed, waving good bye
For the cemetery was closed,
For the night

Constellation of our Own

Millions of people

Zillions of souls

The galaxy

The world

The universe

Yet you stand out

All on your own

Your aura around you

Emitting radiant energy,

Attracting me

Nothing

No one

Nowhere

Can get in our way

For we are our own constellation

For you

The attraction

The magnet

The destiny

Are mine

Our hearts met

With such force

True love rang out

Forming stars

In our own constellation

What is Love?

Love
What is love?
I wonder

Whom to trust?
Not family
Not friends
Not even lover

As fast as
Love can come,
As fast as
Love can go

Tears streaming down my face
For life has lost its purpose
People are not to be trusted
And I hurt so much

Harsh words traded
Physical blows, mind shattering
Faith and trust are broken
All down the drain

Love.

What is love?

I wonder.

My Love Have Left

You are my love
My best friend
My life
My world
My everything

All of a sudden, it was all gone
Before I could even begin to comprehend
Sensitivity, consideration, loyalty, partnership,
Trust, honesty, and especially love
They were all gone in mere seconds

Slipped through my fingers
In my heart, they had heavily set
The tears kept on coming
My love, my adoration,
My world, my idol, my hero

The world has turned vicious
Especially the person who I thought of
As my family, my lover,
My confidant, my role model
Has turned out to be so cruel and ugly

Harsh words traded, all emotionally shattering
She stood far away, all cold and aloof
As I wept, and drowned, in the sea of my misery
My lost love, my sense of stability, my view on people
All had been flushed out by mere air of her bitter coldness

Large crowds had formed, in my support,
Holding up my back, when I really wanted to die
For through years of being with someone, loving someone,
being loved in returned, and loyalty,
I was abandoned of love, my dignity,
and my sense of reality
And the only thing I have left now are my friends...

Why? I struggled, sobbed, and screamed in frustration
Trying to understand,
to make sense of this waking nightmare
How could she? How could the love of my life,
my partner of over five years,
How could she dismiss our life together, our experiences, our
memories, our love
My heart has been shattered, as it has never before,
my love has left...

She was my love
She was my best friend
She was my life
She was my world

She was my everything

168

Cloudy Skies

No matter how hard I tried in vain
To trick this mind of mine
Into its' submissive state, and to relax

However you, as a dark cloud,
Kept on creeping over my head in the sky
Reminding my heart of its' broken state

My tears, they kept on coming, fast and steadily
Mourning of what I had lost
My greatest love, my world had cracked

My eyes dart upward, begging for some comfort
As the dark, cloud-covered sky of loneliness
Tugged at my heart, for the moon was nowhere to be seen

Time, I cried out in frustration, trying to understand
"Heals all wounds," and to "move on"
My soul has broken in half, and you got a half

Where was destiny? Where was fate?
Where did they both go? Off with the moon
Enhancing another world, of a new life

Leaving behind me, a lost and crazed lover

For my heart, you are what it desires

As you bring happiness, brightness and the moon

Dazed and Dead

Living in a world
With a badly broken heart
Whereas everything
Cried out her name
A single memory, a powerful trigger
My world, my life, my future
All seemed so trivial and so empty

I strut on, with nearly empty fuel
Whereas in every shadow, she lives
A piece of furniture, a quote of love
They all bled her name
My heart cried mournfully with each beat
Recognizing the sudden void in my life,
My soul fighting to escape this world

I walk around, dazed and dead, on Earth
The empty half of me echoed her name
My emotionless face, my tense body,
Drugs and friends has become my world
Burying career, school, and life
For my eyes craved for, and saw only her
I am dazed and dead, of heartbreak

Illusion?

And to think
We shared a life
Now I look at you,
Your cold, dispassionate face
And I wonder
Was it all an illusion?

And to think
Of all the places we traveled to,
All the times we shared,
Both happy and sad
All the plans, hopes, and dreams
Was it all an illusion?

Not to mention
All those promises, those
Sweet moments of
"I love you"
Now you could barely talk to me
Was it all an illusion?

What about the home
We had created together?

The families we have joined together
And the furkids we have loved and nurtured?
Now my cat had been stolen by you
Was it all an illusion?

We cross paths now and then
And you could barely put together
More than a sentence
And I wonder, was that the same woman I once loved?
Did we once share a life together?
Or was the whole thing an illusion?

Some Bar Therapy

Dark, seedy bar, all brown and musky
where the loyal locals hung out
through the hazy smoke of cigarettes
and bottomless bottles of beer
we sat, long-time comrades, and talked
bantered, gossiped, and drank

a large, middle-aged man, drinking alone
eventually came around, interfering good company
napkins after napkins, he spewed
history, background, education, and career
his bald head, his belt holding in extra weight
a pitiful man, we sat and nodded, our times a-wastin'

stifling a laughter, my friend stood up and mingled,
leaving me to that sad example of a man
I smiled in all the right places, hurrying him along
yet the ink continued to cover the napkins
his past, his residences, his relationships
my nods became robotic as

the threads of my patience loosened
having had enough, I leaned over the bar counter,

and ordered another round of drinks for us all,
turning the table
with my sweet smile, nodding at the man
who took up our time

as his doughy hands fumbled,
pulling wads of bills out of his wallet
the bartender winked, my friend laughed,
and we guzzled down free beer
for that man had paid off his therapy bill,
relieving us from his burdens

This Is What Love Does To Me

Scorned woman I was, swearing off love
Cynical and bitter to the bone until we met
Your almond eyes melted my icy surface
This is what love does to me…

In a rotten mood, I may be sometimes, all bitching
You manage to diffuse all those with a smile
Lifting me up into a sunny sky, soaring high with me
This is what love does to me…

As the clock ticked toward time
I would be graced with your presence once again
My heart races in anticipation and excitement
This is what love does to me…

With all those fairies in the tub
No way can I keep a straight face with you
For you made me laugh every time
This is what love does to me…

The way you wrap your arms around me
Smothering me with hugs and kisses
Bringing out such joy, happiness, and giddiness

This is what love does to me...

You allow me to be purely myself
No inhibitions, no restrictions, no judgement
All the laughter, silliness, and imitations we shared
This is what love does to me...

My quirks, my habits, my flaws, my passions
You embraced them all without conditions
Accepting me wholly, not only outside, but inside
This is what love does to me...

We dance to the same beats, the same tunes
Finding delight and wonder in everything together
Be it on the road, or in bed, or at a beach
This is what love does to me...

Converted this woman into a believer of love, you did
My heart, you have, on a silver platter, all just for you only
I'm yours, my almond eyes, as long as the earth keeps on
turning
This is what you do to me...

Meeting the Sky

No matter how far apart we are in miles,
We still share the very same sky
The stars you make wishes upon
Are the ones that twinkle high above me
The moon you lay your eyes on and smile
Is the very same one that watch over me while I sleep
Trees, lakes, rivers, highways and roads
They all may stretch out eternally
Putting miles between us, separating us
As the sky condolence us with it's presence
Keep your eyes up, on the dazzling enigmatic sky,
For they carry millions of messages of love and dreams
The sun, the moon, the stars, all that you are to me
In that diamond-filled sky, we dance with joined hands
Awaiting for Mother Earth to catch up, to turn and turn
Until the earth finally meet the sky

Scoot Away, Men

We don't need no jimmies
No ol' mean stinkin' sausages
No ugly, long schlongs
Nor do we need any damn human shaft
Our tool will do just fine

Those lil' soldiers can keep marching on
And my mama always told me no one-eyed-monster existed
And to this day, I still believe her
And remember my phobia of snakes?
Why the heck would I torture myself with a human one?

Joysticks went out years ago, didn't they realize?
Now I've got my Switch and I surely as heck ain't giving it up
As for Jack-in-the-Box, I've gotten over my oral phase
So, keep your Dicks, your Willies and your Larrys away
For I dislike children

Tempting me with your little pony will not work
And don't pull that "better than chocolate" crap on me
For I may be a diva, but I don't do them
So why don't you play Captain Winkie and sail off into sunset
And leave me to me and my women

That Awful Morning

waking up to a sunny morning
hopping out of the shower of a motel
only to find a dreaded text message
from my baby sister...

dad thinks mom is dead
dad thinks?!
he thinks?!
and mom is dead?!

no way! we rush
past all those vehicles
toward our parents' apartment
mom is dead? no way. no.

entering the apartment
dad and sister looked at us helplessly
as mom was laying there, sleeping
looking more at peace than ever

i checked her pulse
only to feel my own heartbeats
i then looked at her closely

letting my heartbeats take over

i turned to my love for assurance
yes, she said with such sadness in her eyes
she is dead. she is gone. look at her
she looks more at peace than ever

I sadly went over to wake up
my other baby sister to deliver
the bad news, mom is gone
she sat up and rubbed her eyes in disbelief

we all stood around in a daze
as the nurse arrived and pronounced mom dead.
it's real? it's true? it's impossible...
tears slid down our cheeks

after we kissed her good bye,
the men came, zipped her up in a bag, and took her away
everyone at loss for words, even though
we were prepared, we were caught unprepared

the sky was so sunny, heaven had gained an angel
mom is free and happy, painless we know
someday we will reunite and be a family once again
yet i will never forget that awful morning

The Ugly Reality

Thinking back to the times,
All those moments of ups and downs
During those unexpected weeks

Mom in the hospital
Then getting out, then back in
And out once again, and then back in

Until the doctors and specialists
Could not do any more
Tests, dialysis and medication

In the end, her body simply gave up
For it tired from years of treatment
All the pain, suffering and restrictions

Now it is seven months later
Since the Lord had called her home
Everything is still so crystal clear

Her hospital bed in the middle
Of the living room, the sun
Filtering through the half-drawn blinds

Hitting my mother
As we all stood there
Scared and helpless

Time was ticking away, and we were
Losing our Mom, Dad his wife,
Grams her daughter, and Aunts and Uncles their sister

This whole thing was nothing but
An awful, surreal nightmare
My throat still constrict at every memory

The lazy chair by mom's hospital bed
In the living room, and the couch
Where my partner and I took turns sleeping on

My hands clasped with Mom's
Fearing of her passing overnight while I slept
Wishing I could hear

Watching the clock and setting alarms to administer
Halogen, morphine and all kind of medication
That would make an addict deliriously happy

Weeks and weeks, ups and downs
With false hope and assumptions
The doctors could save her

Only to discover the ugly reality

That nobody and nothing

Last forever

Like Mother, Like Daughter

I saw the sadness
In your blue eyes
When you admitted
You did ask God
To reunite you
With your departed Dad

I look at my reflection in the mirror
At my blue eyes, only shades lighter,
With the same deep sadness
As I asked, once again,
For God to reunite me
With you, my Mom

When you died,
My heart was torn in two
One was filled with deep heartache
Which seems to intensify over the years
And the other half died along with you,
Cold, hard, black and gone

At your funeral,
I silently prayed with guilt

For God to come and get me
Like He did with you
"Why" was never a question I asked, but
"When?"

I walk around
Like a dead soul
Biding my time on earth
While at nights, I lay awake with emotions
Out of control, wondering where you went
And how badly I want to be with you

Waiting

why do I hurt so bad?
waiting for God's hands
to come and lead me
up above to where Mom is

outside I yell and scream
inside I am crying hysterically
outside I put up a cold front
inside I am a sobbing mess

the world is dark and pointless
people claim to care and love
when they are out only for themselves
around people and in crowds, I feel so alone

time is ticking away, I am not getting any younger
in my bed, I hide out all day long
wishing away my existence and wanting to die
no purpose, no desire, no goals, simply nothingness

my mind, all jumbled up
my emotions, all screwed up
the only thing I know for certain

is I cannot go on living this way

waiting is getting to be too old and too much for me to handle
I need to get out of bed and out of the house
or else I would be leading my own hand
instead of God's and my Mom, whom I may never see ever
again

So Wrong

I thought
Some people were good
With keeping promises

But never have I
Been so wrong,
And it sucks

I thought love
Was to prevail all
And knew no boundaries

But never have I
Been so wrong
And it hurts

I thought wedding vows
Were meant to be
Forever

But never have I
Been so wrong
And it kills

When you looked into my eyes
And told me if anyone was to leave this relationship,
It would have been me

But never have I
Been so wrong
Into believing you

To have and to hold,
For better, for worse
For richer, for poorer

And in sickness
In health,
Till death does us part

But never have I
Been so wrong
By blinding believing those vows

I was your wife,
Yet you disregarded me so easily
And it is heart-shattering

Now, trust
What is that? I question
For I have been so wrong so far

For You Hearing Service Providers

Just because I cannot hear,

And cannot speak your language,

Even though I master at reading and writing in your language,

You don't even know nor understand my damn language

You expect me to read your damn lips,

Forcing me to play guessing games,

And let's throw in some fun

A damn beard, a damn mustache, or a damn accent

Your lips move fast and uncomprehendingly

Or you exaggerate your mouth movement,

Making this educated woman feel like an imbecile

Even though my IQ may be way over yours

You force me to sit all day long, and like an idiot

Giving me the hand, telling me to wait

While you all scamper around,

Figuring out how to deal with me

My rights are being denied,

Accommodations don't happen on time

And we had to keep on educating you all

On simple legal matters, my language, and my culture

Did you forget why I was there in the first place?
And don't you realize you are pushing me off the cliff
To where I want to fly free
And to be free of you all, and a burden to none

The Dead Puppet Master

You sit behind
That big desk
In your office
Like a puppet master

With pasty, waxy skin
Beaky nose and beady eyes
In an old, dusty suit,
The farm at your hands

From day to day, you run the farm,
The funeral home, and the slaughterhouse
With power we dare not question, and
A dead, black heart

Rearranged the farm, you surely did
Giving people no time nor voice,
Only to throw them into dark stalls
And covering your eyes with a paper

You rewarded the terrible,
Stroked the cows, milked them happily,
Playing the innocent and the good,

Mixing deadly potions together

You gave false hope,
Building and setting us up
For great let-downs
And promised dates came and went

You laugh and coo
With your dead relatives,
Then in the next heartbeat,
It's off to the slaughterhouse for us

You claim you wanted more conversations
Then you are offended, for
Your time is too precious for living things
That the dead need not to be bothered with

You hide bodies
From your embalmers
Then you spring a last minute funeral on them
The wake, the funeral and the burial

You robbed the funeral directors blind,
Overstepped their power, and chose a heifer
That had no business at a funeral
To run the home

Chaos and mayhem,
Uncertainty and darkness,
Brought them all to the farm, you surely did
You masterful, dead puppet master

A Broken Doll

Broken and empty,
A sad remains of a doll
Dumped,
Unloved and unwanted.

It's face plastered
With a smile
Intend to satisfy
And to keep peace.

It's chest
All hollowed out
Empty of heart,
Of love.

It's mechanics,
Off whacks.
Sometimes the emotions
Come pouring without control.

Other times,
It is just numb.
Dull, void, and dead
Like the doll's future.

Lost in this place
We call life
This doll wanders around
Alone, zombielike and unreal.

So Broken

You took my hand into yours,
"I'm with you all the way."
And before I knew it,
The words that came from your hands
Were nothing but lies.

Do you love me?
Did you love me?
Do you really love me?
Are you in love with me?
And each time, the answer was yes.

Lies, lies, and lies.
At this point, I sit, all sickened
When I thought of all the lies
You have spewed, and all that I believed
What a dumb fool in love, I was.

Even after you split us up,
Taking away two dogs and two cats,
I still thought highly of you, and I still loved you
Even still, you had my heart
Yet you never appreciated it, and you spit on it.

You turned into a person who I never thought you were,
A liar, a sneak, and someone who could
Never really communicate openly and maturely
Someone who could never really own up
To her misdoings and be a real woman.

And now, you treat me with disrespect,
Treating me differently from others,
I could not wrap my mind around how you chose to cherish those
As opposed to me, someone who you shared twelve years with
Your priorities are definitely out of whack

And when I asked
What exactly was the breaking point?
What was it that broke us?
And to this day,
You still could not give me a direct, clear answer

I've had to walk on eggshells around you,
Dancing around my words, in fear of pissing you off
Which would ensure you to block me,
Cut me out of your life, and cutting all the ties between us
Everything've gotta be your way and your time, or else

Life, as I have known it, for the past twelve years
Felt like nothing but a big lie
Just another sick game life decided to throw my way

And see how far it took to break me
Life, congratulations, you win.

For.

I.

Am.

So.

Broken.

That One Late Afternoon

That one late afternoon
I will never forget

For it was the day
When I was hit with the realization
That no matter how well you think you knew someone,
That person could turn out to be a complete stranger
The sky was gloomy, and everything looked so gray
My eyes were following the blue vehicle in front of me
As I drove in my black Hyundai after work,
My mind going many miles an hour
And that vehicle turned left,
And before my mind had time to process,
I saw it hit a man and that man flipped around
Before he hit the ground, I quickly turned my eyes away
Like I told you,

That one late afternoon,
I will never forget

Panic started to overwhelm me
As I frantically tried to FaceTime that driver
To tell her of what had just taken place,
My trembling finger kept on jabbing at my iPhone
Finally she answered

"What?" she stated, as I blurted out
"You hit a man!" I managed
"You hit a man!"
She mumbled something about a mirror
Yet she kept on driving
My body was shaking with shock, my hands were sweating
profusely
As I called her back "You hit a man!" I repeated, nearly in a full
panic mode
Like I told you,

That one late afternoon,
I will never forget

And she drove onto a McDonald's parking lot
Side by side, we parked our vehicles
I jumped out "You hit a man!" I kept on repeating,
Assuming that we would go back and check on him
"The side mirror flew into my lap," she stated with a cross face
"It was because you hit a man with your car!" I said
"Oh, stop being so dramatic!" she said heatedly
And she turned and walked into McDonald's
I tagged behind her, beyond desperation
Was that man OK? I fretted to myself
"You hit that man!" I told her again,
And scanned my eyes around McDonald's
Like I told you,

That one late afternoon,
I will never forget

And it was when I spotted a policeman, his black uniform
standing out
Here to order dinner, I assumed, yet my legs shook so hard
I turned to her, and there she was, ordering dinner
As if nothing had happened
I felt like I was in some kind of a bad movie
And she was like a killer who had just murdered people
And then got raving hungry after the spree
Who is she? Who was she? My stomach had liquidated
With dinner in bags in our hands, we walked out of
McDonald's
Only to see police vehicles barricading her vehicle
We have been found out already! I felt so sick
And my heart sank all the way to my stomach
Like I told you,

That one late afternoon,
I will never forget

As she walked toward them cooly, acting as if it was just
another day
The policemen started their line of questioning
And they started asking me questions too
Before I knew it, she was laughing with the cops, which fucked
my mind even more
No information on that man have been shared, and to this very

day,
I still wonder about him and what had happened with him
As for her, she had become a scary carbon copy of
Someone who I used to be very close with, and who I used to
know
It was like I got a glimpse into the mind
Of a killer, or of a person with a bottomless black heart
Without any care or remorse for humankind
And it was really scary as fuck, scarier than any scary movies
Like I told you,

That was one late afternoon,
I will never ever forget

Don't Forget Me

Don't forget me
I now know you won't

You may have forgotten
Like I have
For over thirty years,
It was all locked away

Until that day
When I saw you,
And it all came
Flooding back

Fuck you
For traumatizing me
In my youth
And for disrespecting me

Fuck you
For violating my young body
And for ruining my innocence
I had to live for years with a heavy secret

Fuck you
For acting like nothing happened
And for thinking that
You could have me years later

Fuck you
For thinking you could change my identity
When I have repeatedly told you
I am a lesbian

Fuck you
For having weak balls
And for being a coward,
Sending an ugly whore of a bitch to fight for you

And I sit here thinking about it all now,
Like I have countless of days and nights
And know what?
I can finally say fuck you

I am so glad
I did what I did to you
I am so happy
I royally fucked you over

I hope I traumatized you
With women
Like how you have

Traumatized me

I am finally at peace
With myself,
My conscience is all clean
I have no regrets

I just hope you will
Never ever forget me
For it is your sin
To live with

Don't forget me
I know you won't
And that gives me
A big satisfaction

Fuck you
From that young girl you violated
And fuck you
From this grown woman who now knows her worth

Don't forget me
I now know you won't.

Realization

I got into your car
And upon seeing you,
A huge smile came to my face immediately

I started to struggle
In keeping my face neutral and expressionless
Yet the smile stubbornly spread widely across my face

To the point where I could
Feel my energy pulsating
And filling up your car

You turned to me
And you asked "what?"
With a shy smile

I could not tell you
I could not explain to you
I simply shook my head

You turned your eyes back to the road
The e-cig in your hand,
Your manicured, eggplant colored nails

I still could not wipe
The huge smile off my face
And you turned to me once again

There it was, your smile,
Beautiful and sweet,
As you asked again, "what?"

I could not tell you
I could not explain to you
I shook my head once more

As my heart skipped a beat
My smile about to give it away
And I turned my head away

"A beautiful day." I exclaimed
As you nodded in agreement,
Your right hand on the steering wheel

I could not tell you now
I could not explain to you now
But I hope I will be able to soon

Of the reason for my smile,
For you are it
As my heart had just realized something

Don't Give Me the Hand

I may be Deaf,

And I am not able to speak your language

Even though I can read, write, and understand your language
fluently,

Whereas most of you don't understand ours,

Or even come close to it

When I approach you,

Please maintain eye contact

When I ask a question,

Please look into my eyes and

Give me an answer

Do not tell me to sit down

And then avert your eyes to block out

Any possibility of communication

Get me a paper and a pen if needed,

Or type it out on a phone

You can also gesture,

Point at, or ask someone else to help out

Or try anything to make communication

Easier and possible

When there's a will, there's a way

But do not treat me as if I was stupid,
And do not give me the hand
Which was to silence me
And do not treat me like a child
Or an uneducated person

Do not give me the hand
For audism and ableism are
Tightly tied to your non-signing hand,
And I am so ready to cut it off
For I am tired of being treated this way

What Is It?

What is it
About you
That had stirred
Something very deep
Within me?

I cannot even
Begin to comprehend
Or explain all of this
Feelings I am experiencing
And it is driving me crazy.

What is it
About you
That had gotten me
Thinking about you
Constantly?

You have literally
Taken over my mind
For some reason,
And I am trying to
Figure out how that happened.

What is it
About you
That made me want to
Just throw caution to the wind
And rush toward you?

Instead, I sit here
Trying to restrain
My mind and my emotions
From running amok
And to make sense of them all.

What is it
About you
That had somehow
Set my heart
On fire?

Your smile, your laughter,
The way you sign,
Your beauty, your thoughts,
Your words, your energy
I keep wanting more.

What is it
About you

That got me
All wound up and flustered
Like a love-struck teenager?

I really also have no idea
How you feel about me,
And how to define
What is going on between us.
What is it about you?

A Wildfire

Like a wildfire, fast and raging,
You have consumed every area of my brain
Before I even began to realize

I miss steps, I drop things,
Drive through stop signs,
And zone out on conversations

You occupy my every thought,
Manifesting it's way deep
Into far-away places that were untouched for years

I wake up in the mornings
And I go to sleep at nights
With you on my mind

Our video conversations, I enjoy tremendously
Your text messages bring both
Smiles and blushes to my face

My mood, my energy
They all radiate like the sun
All because of you

You have ignited
A big spark in me,
Awakening the fire
216

And now this fire
Is leading me toward you
Hot and fast, like a wildfire

For Now

Months and months
Of daily connections through technology
Messages, pictures, video messages, and video calls

I hang in onto your every word,
Soaking in what I can of you
Through conversations, pictures, videos and dreams

Kept apart by distance
One thousand one hundred twelve miles, to be exact
And not to mention stuff in life, one after another

And finally, there you were
In the flesh, beyond my wildest imagination
Making my dreams reality

The way you leaned over, your blue eyes deep into mine,
Making the whole world melt away
As your luscious lips lock on mine

And with you in my bed at nights
With our arms and legs all tangled,
It was too surreal, you being present

The meals we shared, the talks, the laughs,
Holding hands and walking around
And yes, the baths too

You have struck some heavy chords in me,
Both of fear and realization,
For my heart, you have deeply captured

And now we are back at it again with technology,
The distance and life tearing at my very soul
For I so very much want to be with you

Instead, I resign myself for the time being
To messages, pictures, video messages and video calls,
Relying on your words until we connect again in person

About the Author

Rose Ann Goodman "Rosey" is a native Deaf and lesbian Pennsylvanian who spent most of her 30's and 40's in Texas, where she currently lives with her dog, Lulu and her kitty, Rhyme. She has won writing awards and published poetry in anthologies. This is her first book of poetry.